FAST JETS 2

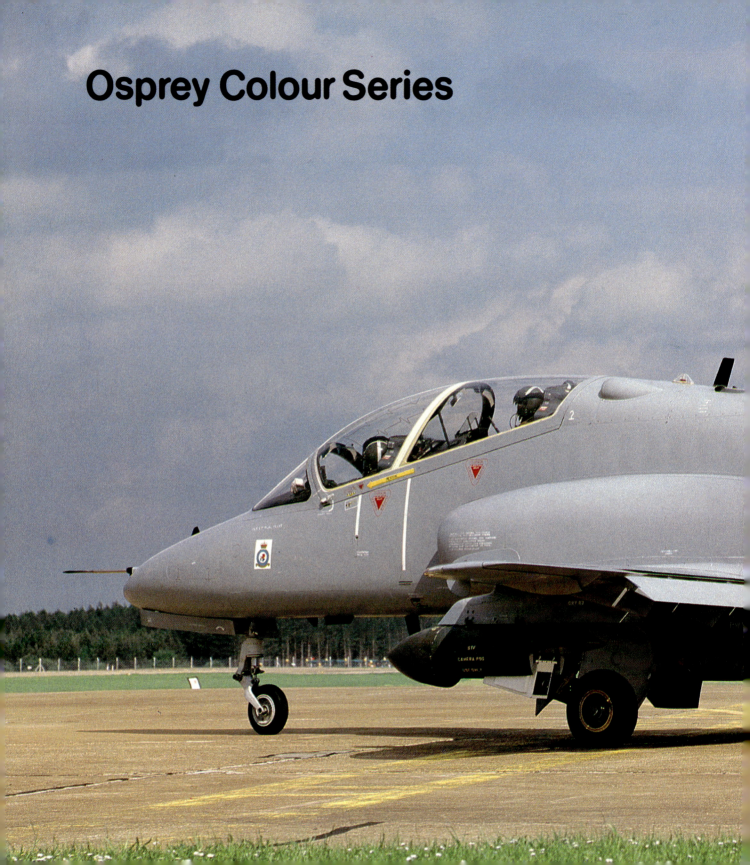

Osprey Colour Series

FAST JETS 2

Chris Allan

Published in 1987 by Osprey Publishing Limited
27A Floral Street, London WC2E 9DP
Member company of the George Philip Group

British Library Cataloguing in Publication Data

Allan, Chris
  Fast jets, 2. — (Osprey colour series)
  1. Fighter planes — Pictorial works
  2. Jet planes, Military — Pictorial works
  I. Title
  623.74'64 UG1242.F5

ISBN 0-85045-754-8

Editor Dennis Baldry
Designed by David Tarbutt
Printed in Hong Kong

Right A Lightning F.6 of No 11 Sqn leads a pair of
F-15C Eagles into the sunset during a recovery to
Binbrook in December 1986. The Eagles belong to
the 32nd Tactical Fighter Squadron based at
Soesterberg in the Netherlands. Both Eagles are
carrying a centreline 600 US gal (2270 lit) combat-
rated fuel tank

After the enthusiastic response to his first book, *FAST JETS — A pilot's eye view* published by Osprey in March 1986, Lightning pilot Flight Lieutenant Chris Allan was commissioned to produce a follow-up. *FAST JETS 2* is that book. As these words are written, Chris Allan is still flying as a Qualified Weapons Instructor (QWI) with the Lightning Training Flight (LTF) at Binbrook in Lincolnshire, but this unit will cease to exist on 16 April 1987. In August 1987 Chris Allan is leaving the Royal Air Force to pursue a career in civil aviation.

During his association with the Lightning Chris Allan has flown the aircraft at Mach 2 on several occasions, and reached Mach 1.8 in the T.5 two-seater. He has fired a number of Firestreak and Red Top air-to-air missiles from various Lightnings and observed Sidewinder AAMs fired by other types of aircraft. In the course of air combat training the author has tangled with virtually every fighter and strike/attack aircraft in the NATO inventory, including the Mirage family, Phantom, Tornado, F-15 Eagle, F-16 Fighting Falcon, and US Navy F-14 Tomcats over the Mediterranean. His log book records over 1500 hr on type.

Once again, this book would not have been possible without the generous help of many individuals. Lack of space makes a collective 'thank you' inevitable, but the author would like to record his sincere gratitude to everyone who assisted. *FAST JETS 2* was shot using Rolleiflex cameras and lenses loaded with Fuji and Kadochrome film. All of the air-to-air photographs were taken during normal training flights. The views expressed in this book are the author's and do not necessarily reflect those of the Ministry of Defence or of the Royal Air Force.

Front cover This is believed to be the first picture ever published of a Lockheed SR-71 Blackbird jettisioning its unique JP-7 fuel — the vent is located in the boat-tail section of the rear fuselage. The SR-71 is operated exclusively by the 9th Strategic Reconnaissance Wing, 1st Strategic Reconnaissance Squadron of the US Air Force, based at Beale AFB in sunny California. Detachments are stationed at Kadena (Det 1) on the Japanese island of Okinawa, and RAF Mildenhall (Det 4) in Suffolk, England. This particular SR-71A was photographed in the vicinity of Mildenhall in the summer of 1986 using Rolleiflex camera equipment mounted in a CBLS (carrier bomb light stores) pod under the left wing of the British Aerospace Hawk T.1A illustrated on the **title pages**. The Hawk picture is courtesy of **Air Portraits**. Flt Lt 'Spike' Newberry (currently flying the 'Red Four' slot in the Red Arrows aerobatic team) piloted the Hawk camera ship (XX317) during the Blackbird, and other photo-sorties. The camera pod system is remotely-controlled by the author from the Hawk's rear cockpit

Back cover The author seated in the rear cockpit of a Belgian Air Force F-16B from No 350 Sqn, Beauvechain, during the eight-nation Tactical Fighter Meet held at RAF Waddington, Lincolnshire, in August 1986. Coded FB-12, this aircraft carries a Gaul's head badge on the fin

Right A classic shock-wave frames a Buccaneer S.2D maritime strike aircraft of Lossiemouth-based No 208 Sqn crewed by Flt Lt Tony Burtenshaw and navigator Flt Lt Clive Lambourne. A week later I had my sight on Tony's Buccaneer when he pulled up and declared a 'PAN' (emergency) during a low-level affliliation sortie over the North Sea. Had I actually shot him? No, the Bucc's starboard engine had taken a bird at over 500 knots — it must have caused a bit of a jolt. The bird had ripped into the intake wall on its way through and the engine was severely damaged. Fortunately Binbrook was close at hand and Tony diverted there, giving me the chance to discuss the real 'kill' with him over a beer that evening

Contents

Blackbird encounter

It is difficult to believe that this mysterious, futuristic shape first flew as long ago as 22 December 1964. But it certainly did, reaching Mach 1.5 before presiding test pilot Robert J Gilliland brought the SR-71 prototype back to Palmdale, Calfornia. Since then Lockheed's Mach 3 hot-shot has been in action over Vietnam, Laos, Cuba, and a host of other trouble-spots around the world. At its maximum operating speed and altitude the SR-71 is unlikely to be intercepted by anything in the arsenal of most countries, and even potent adversaries like the Soviet MiG-31 are going to have a hard time splashing one. **Above** Only the left-hand inlet spike, engine nacelle, and outer wing of the SR-71 are visible as it holds station behind the Hawk camera ship

9

Sun glinting off the canopy strut, the SR-71 looms into tight formation. The back seater — actually a reconnaissance systems officer (RSO), to give him his full title — has two small windows (barely visible in this view) and a ventral periscope to enjoy a sight of the outside world when he isn't too busy operating cameras and highly classified electronic equipment. An Elint (electronic intelligence) panel is discernible under the chine

The Hawk has been flown supersonically in a 60 degree dive during the course of test flying (at a True Mach Number of 1.1 to be exact) which isn't bad for what is basically a two-seat advanced trainer. But the SR-71 is obviously in a class of its own, capable of sustaining Mach 3.2 or 2112 mph (3340 km/h) for long periods at altitudes in excess of 82,000 ft (25,000 m). The fact that this speed and altitude performance is almost a matter of routine (some 'Mach 2' combat aircraft rarely venture beyond subsonic speeds) is testimony to the care and sophistication that goes into preparing a Blackbird mission and the outstanding flying qualities of the aircraft

Overleaf Even the worst exponent of aircraft recognition can't fail to identify (I hope!) the unmistakable outline of the Blackbird from this distance — it might be a little trickier when the aircraft is operating in the upper region of its flight envelope. Incidentally, the Blackbird is known as the 'Habu' by aircrews and associated personnel, a tradition stretching back to the first SR-71 deployment to Kadena air base on the Japanese island of Okinawa in 1968, when the locals named the menacing black machine after an indigenous species of pit viper

Looking strangely out-of-place above a patchwork of English fields and woodland, the SR-71 is happier in the rarified dark blue skies at the furthest reaches of the Earth's atmosphere, vulnerable to nothing except technical problems and 'smart' surface-to-air missiles, perhaps terminally guided by infrared

Blackbird break: despite its size (103.83 ft [31.65 m] along, 55.58 ft [16.94 m] span), the SR-71 can be flown with considerable élan at subsonic speeds, as many satisfied airshow crowds will testify. Its *pièce de résistance* has to be the thrilling spectacle of a simulated engine out approach and flyby, full afterburner and hard opposite rudder balancing the loss of thrust from the 'dead' J58. Apart from the superb piloting involved, this display emphasizes the SR-71's enviable low-speed controllability

A pair of mighty Pratt & Whitney J58 turbojets, each rated at 32,500 lb (14,742 kg) in afterburner at sea level, dominate the airframe and burn about 8000 US gal (30,303 lit) of JP-7 per hour at maximum speed. The engine only produces 17.6 per cent of the total thrust at Mach 3.2, the inlet and ejector accounting for 54 and 28.4 per cent respectively. Clever stuff...

Right Bye Bye Blackbird: accelerating into the ether

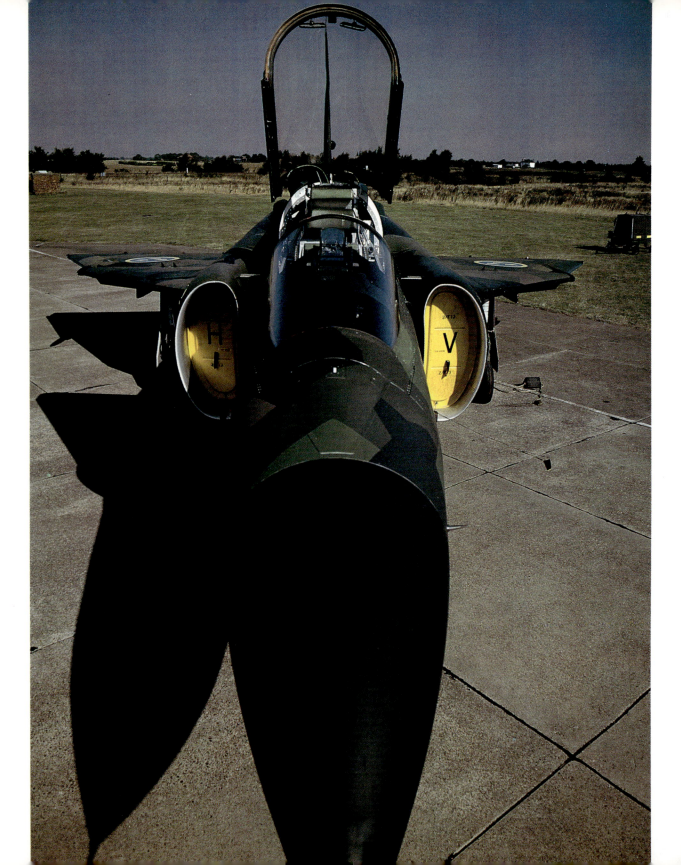

Thunderbolt and Thunderclap

Left The Viggen, literally translated as 'the hammer blow of Thor' (Thunderclap is close enough) is one of the world's outstanding warplanes. Designed as an integral part of Sweden's STRIL 60 defence system, the Saab Viggen has show-stopping STOL (short takeoff and landing) performance, operating with a decent warload from tight 500 m (1640 ft) strips that are off-limits to comparable combat aircraft. This Viggen is one of 141 JA37 interceptors ordered by the *Flygvapnet* and it serves with No 2 Sqn of the F13 wing based at Norrköping, 95 miles (150 km) south-west of Stockholm

Despite being called Thunderbolt II by manufacturer Fairchild after the aircraft's illustrious piston-engined forbear (the P-47, or 'Jug') everyone calls the tank-busting A-10 the 'Warthog' because it's so goddam ugly. This example is one of around 120 in service with the 81st Tactical Fighter Wing at the twin bases of Bentwaters and Woodbridge in Suffolk, England. A total of 713 A-10s were delivered to the US Air Force and production is complete

Above This is the view a MIG-driver will probably see if he's tempted to tangle with a Warthog down in the weeds. The 'Hog can turn on a dime and although the pilot's sighting system is optimized for air-to-ground firing, the seven-barrel Avenger cannon can be used to rip open fast-jets, too. But the really bad news is that A-10s are now able to carry four Sidewinders on the outboard pylons for self-defence and anti-helicopter roles. The smart play is to bug out (disengage) if you can't kill an A-10 on the first pass. **Left** The A-10's warpaint blends in nicely against typical European scenery. **Right** Capt Sean Jessurun, A-10 display pilot for 1986, waits for taxi clearance before the start of his routine at the Mildenhall Open Day

A head-on view of the Viggen: the kidney-shaped intakes supply air to the Volve Flygmotor RM8B turbofan, a version of the civil Pratt & Whitney JT8D fitted with a Swedish-designed afterburner and thrust reverser. The RM8B develops 28,108 lb (12,750 kg) of thrust with reheat. When the aircraft is at rest, the elevons droop from the canard (or foreplane) surfaces, but when the hydraulics come on-line the elevons power-up to adopt the angle determined by the control column. The canards provide the high-lift needed for STOL performance and air-combat agility

Visible above the belly tank, the gas-operated Oerlikon KCA 30 mm cannon is wrapped in a low-drag fairing which also contains the ammunition and feed mechanism. The gun fires 22 rounds per second with twice the effective range and eight times the impact energy of older 30 mm weapons like the Aden or DEFA 5-52. For a typical intercept mission the JA37 Jaktviggen is also armed with two short-range Rb.24 Sidewinder all-aspect infrared homing missiles and two Rb.71 Sky Flash semi-active radar guided missiles. Target illumination for Sky Flash is provided by Ericsson's superb PS-46/A X-band pulse-Doppler radar system

23

All Viggen versions are fitted with a Saab-designed Type 37 zero-zero ejection seat (two for the SK37 tandem trainer), fired by pulling the large handle on top of the headrest. Saab designed their first ejection seat for the J21 fighter which flew in 1943

Right The vertical fin can be folded to squeeze the Viggen in and out of small hangars at dispersed sites. The thrust reverser lids are located in the ejector (below the rudder) and they are automatically actuated by landing gear compression on touchdown. Above Mach 1, with the intake closed, the ejector becomes a supersonic nozzle

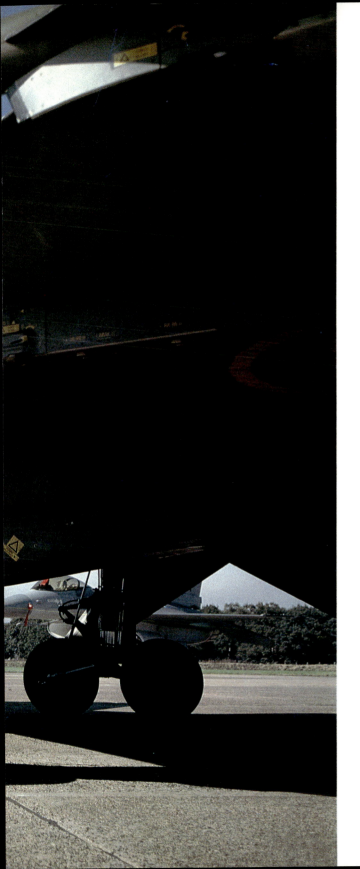

Above Ulf Johansson, 1986 Viggen display pilot, dismounts after his dramatic demonstration to the crowds at RAF Finningley near Doncaster in September, during which he made an unbelievably short landing followed by a backward 360-degree turn using reverse thrust and nosewheel steering. Follow that! **Left** From this angle it's not difficult to see why actor/director Clint Eastwood wanted to use a Viggen to represent the high-tech Soviet superfighter in his motion picture *Firefox*. It didn't work out though, and he had to use some rather dodgy special effects instead. The projections forward of the wing house the radar homing and warning system (RHAWS)

Lightning valedictory

Left Photographed by fellow Lightning pilot Flt Lt Ian Black, the author pulls into a vertical climb in full reheat shortly after takeoff — the classic 'rote' admired by Lightning groupies everywhere. Due to the high humidity the water vapour being forced out of the atmosphere indicates the turbulent airflow over the wings during this part of the manoeuvre

Above Armament Practice Camp (APC) at Akrotiri, Cyprus: Lightning ammo tanks are ready for uploading from the gun trolley

If you don't like Lightnings the next 28 pages are going to be pretty boring. I make no apology for including so many Lightning shots — indeed, editor Dennis Baldry insisted that I should — because what is almost certainly the last (and only!) single-seat supersonic fighter of wholly British design and manufacture to see RAF service has been an endangered species for many years, and extinction is scheduled for the spring of 1988. **Left** Back in Cyprus, the linked 30 mm rounds for the two Aden revolver cannons are being connected in 30-round belts. Each ammo tank holds a maximum of 240 rounds, supplying 120 rounds to each gun. **Right** For target practice the shells are dipped in different coloured dyes to differenciate between the scores of each pilot by making a distinctive mark as they whizz through the white banner target

Armourers download the empty ammo tanks from a Lightning F.6 of No 11 Sqn during an operational turnround (OTR). The soot produced by departing shells is clearly visible downstream of the left-hand cannon port (extreme left)

The same aircraft (XR758) receives attention from the two 'plumbers' tasked with ensuring that no rounds are left in either gun breech if the guns have not been 'fired-out' — which takes 6 seconds at 1200 rounds per minute — or become jammed. The Adens are harmonized to concentrate their firepower at a range of 375 yards (343 m), although an attack can be pressed home until debris from the target becomes a real hazard

This Lightning F.6 from No 11 Sqn needs to be flown at a high angle of attack (AOA) to maintain formation on the somewhat slower Canberra (WT519) target facilities aircraft operated by No 100 Sqn

Not content to hold station on the Canberra tug, the Lightning moves astern for a close look at the banner, a 6 ft × 30 ft (1.5 m × 9 m) target made of woven hessian. This particular banner came from a batch which had the 'black dot' printed on upside down. The banner can't be flown the other way up because the spreader bar is weighted to pull it with the dot uppermost

The author (on banner) assesses individual marksmanship during an APC back in 1983. This is where the Bravo Sierra stops — irrespective of rank and experience the scores tell all

A Firestreak-armed 'Tub', better known as the Lightning T.5 two-seat operational trainer, recovers to Binbrook in company with Lightning F.3 'Delta Bravo' (also toting Firestreaks in background) from the Lightning Training Flight. This was a memorable sortie for Flt Lt Craig Penrice in 'Alpha Zulu' with QFI (Qualified Flying Instructor) and 1986 Lightning display pilot Sqn Ldr John Aldington. Ten months earlier Craig had been forced to eject from a Lightning F.6 after it developed a severe control restriction. Since restored to full flying duties, Craig's long lay-off was a result of the major injuries he sustained to his right arm on the way out. That's my refuelling probe in the foreground

37

Left Reefing into the vertical at 25,000 ft (7620 m) after a two-minute climb from 250 ft (75 m) with Flt Lt 'Porky' Page off my right wing. Its spine and fin painted deep blue, this Lightning F.3 (XR749/DA) is specially adorned to mark the 10th anniversary of the LTF (1 October 1985)

Above Another view of F.3 'Delta Bravo' (XP707), this time highlighted by the setting sun at the end of the day's flying. The F.3 entered RAF squadron service with No 74 (Tiger) Sqn at Leuchars, Scotland, on 14 April 1964

Overleaf Representatives of every air defence squadron in No 11 Group, RAF, lined up at Mildenhall to mark the 50th anniversary of the formation of Fighter Command (14 July 1936). Lightnings to the fore, with Phantoms and Hawks beyond

A nine-ship from No 5(F) Sqn ('The Fighting Fifth') led by Wg Cdr Andy Williams' distinctive red-finned F.6 celebrate their 21st year of continuous operation with the Lightning in October 1986

At the heart of the action, astern the nine-ship
formation

Twilight recovery: 'Delta Foxtrot', an LTF F.6, heads back to Binbrook. This particular aircraft, XR726, is used as a high-speed target for practice interception work. A non-standard fuel tank replaces the gunpack to gain an extra 800 lb (363 kg) of precious fuel

Inset Flt Lt Bob Bees of No 11 Sqn prepares to fly again after his copybook ejection from Lightning XR760/BL, which crashed into the North Sea off Whitby on 15 July 1986 after succumbing to a reheat fire — the 79th Lightning loss in some 26 years of operation. Surprisingly, Bob was fit for flying duties almost immediately after his parachute ride, but he was detained for observation just in case. Plans to retrofit the Lightning fleet with the excellent Martin-Baker Mk 10 zero-zero ejection seat fell foul of budgetary restrictions

Bottom left Lightning getaway 1: Sqn Ldr John Aldington blasts off in F.3 XP764/DC at the beginning of a practice display

Below Lightning getaway 2: closer, main gears tucking away, an F.6 from No 11 Sqn takes off from Runway 03 at Binbrook. The revised 'kinked' wing leading edge and bigger ventral tank distinguishes the F.6 from the gunless F.3 variant

With parabrake and airbrakes deployed, Sqn Ldr John Aldington brings F.3 XP764/DC down the runway at the end of his practice routine. Back in 1973-74, John Aldington flew with the Jet Provost-mounted Macaws and Swords aerobatic display teams, based at Manby (since closed) and Leeming respectively. He is currently a flight commander on No 11 Sqn

Not a still from the motion picture *Star Wars*, but the author at work in the cockpit of a Lightning F.3. The wide-angle lens accentuates the heavy canopy framing and visibility from the cockpit is not nearly as bad as this view suggests. However, in common with other fighters of its era such as the Mirage III and MiG-21, rear-vision is very restricted

Vortices streaming from their wingtips, a
three-ship of F.6s from Binbrook head for the
Open Day at Mildenhall in May 1986. The leader is
XS923/DF of the LTF flown by Flt Lt Dave Hart,
flanked by XS929/BG of No 11 Sqn (nearest
camera) flown by Flt Lt Paul Field, and XS928/AH
from No 5(F) Sqn piloted by Flt Lt Steve Bridger.
Both wingmen are carrying Firestreaks, while lead
has Red Tops

50

Yes, there are three Lightnings here, tucked in tightly as they turn in echelon port. Like the F.3 before it, the F.6 is powered by a pair of Rolls-Royce Avon 301 turbojets each rated at 16,300 lb (7363 kg) of thrust with reheat

Follow my leader. The Lightning is the fastest
aircraft ever operated by the RAF, capable of 1500
mph (2413 km/h) or Mach 2.3 at altitude, and the
swiftest climber at an initial rate of 50,000 ft
(15,240 m) per minute

As tactically useless today as it was in 1940, vic
formation is strictly reserved for special occasions
like air displays. The basic combat element is a
two-ship with the wingman covering his leader, a
system developed by the great German ace Werner
Mölders during the Spanish Civil War. He called it
the *rotte*, and suitably updated for jet speeds and
missile launching it still makes sense in the air
combat arena of the 1980s. **Overleaf** Three-ship
finale. The Lightning can still catch almost
anything with wings, but the restrictive launch
envelope of both Firestreak and Red Top make it
practically impossible to kill a highly-manoeuvrable
target in the class of the F-16 (unless its pilot is
asleep). But with a quartet of Sidewinder AIM-9Ls,
the old Lightning would be difficult to beat in close
combat

54

Sunset strip: Binbrook will close as a fighter base when Nos 5 and 11 Sqns re-equip with the Panavia Tornado F.3 air defence variant in 1987-88. It's still 'touch-and-go' at Binbrook as this F.6 climbs away to rejoin the circuit. The Lightning lands at 175 mph (281 km/h) and needs 7500 ft (2286 m) of runway to ensure an adequate safety margin in the event of engine problems or parabrake failure. In a severe crosswind, the aircraft will wear out a set of tyres after a single takeoff and landing

Tactical Fighter Meet

Left Tricky Dicky: an F-16 pilot of No 350 Sqn, Beauvechain, snapped-in to the man-efficient cockpit of his mount. He is gripping the sidestick (left of picture) and throttle which, in addition to their classic functions, are equipped with all the switchology required to operate the radar system, head-up display (HUD), weapons, etc. In other words, he can *fly* and *fight* the Falcon simultaneously

Dispersed parking at RAF Waddington, Lincolnshire, home of 'Tactical Fighter Meet 86' during the week 2-9 August: FB-111As of the 509th Bomb Wing, Strategic Air Command, from Pease AFB, New Hampshire (background), and F-16As of the 474th Tactical Fighter Wing, Nellis AFB, Nevada (left), and the 401st TFW, Torrejon, Spain, share the concrete with RAF refuelling bowsers

Left An F-16A from the 401st TFW waits for its load of inert 500 lb (227 kg) practice bombs. The F-16s were mostly used for ground attack or 'mud-moving' missions, but the Falcon's air combat qualities don't disappear just because you hang bombs on it. Indeed, they still had the edge to beat the packs of role-dedicated 'fighters' sent to intercept them. **Above** F-16 style: discussing the turnround requirements for the next sortie

The F-16's big, beautiful canopy is a fighter pilot's dream

The low-slung intake of the F-16 poses fewer FOD (foreign object damage) problems than one would expect. TFM sortie scenarios changed from muds versus the AD pukes, to escort and offensive sweep profiles. In the latter case, instead of the forces opposing one another, they worked hand-in-hand to challenge the fighter assets of No 11 Group

A Torrejon-based F-16 sporting a black 'Fighting Falcon' motif above the cannon port and blast deflector of its M61A1 Vulcan 20 mm cannon. This widely used six-barrel weapon can fire a maximum of 100 high-velocity shells per second. The average stoppage rate is just one round in 10,000

The F-16 is powered by a Pratt & Whitney F100-200 turbofan rated at 23,840 lb (10,814 kg) of thrust with afterburner. Post-start checks include checking the aircraft's neat split-level airbrakes

Overleaf A pair of Belgian F-16s take off in cold-power. Once they have adjusted to the control sensitivity of the sidestick, pilots prefer it to a traditional, centrally-mounted control column — formation flying is apparently much easier. Belgium has taken delivery of 116 F-16s, and a further 44 will be added from 1988

F-16s J-255 (lead) and J-232 of No 323 Sqn, Royal Netherlands Air Force, depart from Waddinton to maintain CAPs (combat air patrols) over the targets allocated to the muds. Interestingly, after returning to the conversion unit at Leeuwarden, one pilot found himself training the world's first female F-16 jockey

A pilot from Bierset-based No 1 Sqn, Belgian Air
Force, buckles into his Mirage 5BA; the ejection
seat is a Martin-Baker BRM 4. In recent years
Belgian pilots have had to contend with
maddening fuel restrictions, but the situation is
gradually improving

The two-seat Mirage 5BD from No 8 Sqn, Mirage Operational Conversion Unit, in which the author made a 55-minute low-level familiarization flight in battle formation through North Yorkshire, Wales, Cornwall, Devon, and Shropshire before recovering into Waddington. I found the Mirage very heavy in pitch compared to other aircraft, although the electric trim is extremely effective

The Belgian Air Force operates 41 Dassault-
Breguet Mirage 5BAs in the fighter/ground-attack
role. BA03 displays the uncluttered lines of a
thoroughbred

Going for it, low down over the Welsh peat bogs

The Mirage 5 is a simply-equipped version of the Mirage III strike fighter and its pilots have to manage without the trick nav/attack kit fitted to aircraft like the Harrier and Jaguar. If necessary, ground track, targeting, detours and diversions have to be flown 'free nav' using thumb, map and stopwatch. If you have to look in, better watch out — there's bound to be an AD puke lurking about

Now you see them...

...now you don't! Specially posed, this majestic
vic of three Mirages proves just how effective
tactical camouflage can be over urban areas

Airbrakes flipped out, the classic delta planform of the Mirage stares back in a spirited break. Two big 374 Imp gal (1700 lit) fuel tanks are carried to extend low-level operational radius. A flare dispenser (black rectangle) to confuse infrared-guided missiles is fitted near the wing trailing-edge root

Unbuckling at mission's end. Due to bad weather
the Bierset boys had to wait several days before
being cleared to 'famil' over the UK

Mirage muscle: the 5 series is powered by the SNECMA Atar 9C single-shaft turbojet of 13,670 lb (6200 kg) thrust with afterburner. A parabrake is located in the fairing immediately above the engine nozzle

Above Time for the debrief. The Mirage OCU at Bierset has ten 5BD trainers, represented by BD10 in the background. **Right** The author (centre) debriefs F-16 pilots from No 350 Sqn during the course of his staff duties at TFM 86, 350 are AD pukes and do not normally utilize the F-16s inertial navigation system (INS), fitted for low-level offensive strike. However, several of the scenarios in the Meet involved coordinated CAPs which had to be accurately postioned to protect the muds during the run-in and escape from the objective, so the fighter jocks had to 'get in the books' and self-train on the inertial nav kit

Arriving in a characteristically nose-high attitude to maximize aerodynamic braking (the tail-bumper isn't cosmetic) a Saab A-35DX Draken (Dragon), serial A-007, feels for the runway. The four Drakens at TFM 86 came from No 725 Sqn, Royal Danish Air Force, based at Karup. To increase the Draken's effectiveness in the NATO environment of the 1980s and beyond, the Danes have installed new weapon aiming computers, HUDs, RWR, and INS

An immaculate A-35DX parked behind some
rather less well-presented 500 lb (227 kg) low-drag
bombs, or 'slicks'

More rusty bombs, this time retarded 500-pounders. Drag-inducing extendable fins give the pilot enough time to escape the debris hemisphere after a low-level pickle (release). Connected to a ground power source, the aircraft is ready for the day's sortie. Only one mission per day was launched at the TFM — no reflection on the capabilities of the forces involved but deliberate policy. This gave enough time for a thorough evaluation of the scenario brief, sortie brief, the actual mission, and debrief — a long process when the comments of over 100 aircrew have to be correlated. A Sidewinder AAM, fitted with its protective nosecap, is attached to an outboard pylon via a special adaptor

Until recently exports of Saab's clever double-delta
had been limited to Denmark and Finland, but in
May 1985 Austria signed for 24 refurbished
Swedish Air Force J35Ds in preference to the
Lightnings offered by British Aerospace. An
S-35DX reconnaissance machine, serial AR-114,
seeks its element

The war room of an FB-111A from the 509th BW based at Pease AFB, New Hampshire. If the big swinger decides to quit flying the entire cockpit enclosure becomes an escape capsule and the crew descend like returning Apollo Astronauts before being rescued. The escape system is activated by pulling either of the large handles situated between the seats. When the awesome Aardvark is at rest, red-flagged safety-pins ensure the capsule remains part of the airframe. The FB-111A features a Mk IIB all-digital, computer-controlled avionics suite (derived from the system fitted to the F-111D), Doppler and terrain-following radars, an optical display sight and a low-altitude radar altimeter set. Using this equipment, the pilot and his 'whizzo' (weapons systems officer) can penetrate deep into enemy territory day or night, in horrible weather, to deliver up to six AGM-69A SRAMS (short-range attack missiles), or six nuclear bombs, or up to 31,500 lb (14,300 kg) of conventional bombs. No wonder SAC is strong on strike

Strategic Air Command acquired a limited-edition
of 76 FB-111As to replace the mighty Convair
B-58 Hustler. When most of the 132 Northrop B-2
stealth bombers become operational in the mid-
1990s, the remaining FB-111As will be transferred
to Tactical Air Command. The 509th BW caused a
bit of a stir at TFM 86 with their new 'anechoic'
paint scheme, designed to minimize the aircraft's
infrared and radar emissivity. A Sidewinder for
self-defence — a rare sight on a F-111 — is loaded
under the right-hand non-swivelling glove pylon

Top Included for comparison with the FB-111A and EF-111A, a Vietnam-style camouflaged F-111F of the 48th TFW steps on the loud pedal at Lakenheath. This particular aircraft was not included in the force of 18 F-111Fs which set out to bomb the Libyan capital, Tripoli, on 15 April 1986

Left The 42nd Electronic Combat Squadron, 20th Tactical Fighter Wing, based at Upper Heyford in Oxfordshire, provided a pair of their beam-battling EF-111A Ravens to grill the 'enemy' radars on the last day of the Meet. Staying on the subject of paint schemes, the Spark 'Vark's low visibility 'grey ghost' finish makes visual acquisition a troublesome task, especially in heavy cloud cover

A total of 42 EF-111As were remanufactured from standard General Dynamics' F-111A bombers by Grumman Aerospace at their Calverton, New York, facility. The EF-111A features an improved version of the ALQ-99 electronic warfare system used by US Navy EA-6B Prowlers to block, jam, or deceive hostile radars and deflect oncoming SAMs. At present the Raven is unarmed, but the glove pylons may sprout HARMs (high speed anti-radiation missiles) to hit back against ground-based radars. The main body of the AN/ALQ-99E system and its associated jammers is contained in a long 'canoe' radome under the fuselage, backed-up by threat receivers in the large pod atop the fin *à la* Prowler. Not surprisingly, the electronic warfare officer (EWO) in the Raven's right-hand seat is faced with a somewhat different instrument layout to his strike-orientated forbear. The EWO controls the tactical jamming and deception activity by using an advanced CRT digital display indicator and various threat analysers. Jumping back slightly, the bottom picture illustrates the upturned nose shape which earned the F-111 its Aardvark nickname

Raven BEAM 13 en route to its roost at Upper Heyford. The only other US Air Force unit operating the EF-111A is the 390th ECS, 366th TFW, based at Mountain Home AFB, Idaho

Armée de l'Air Sepecat Jaguar As of EC 4/7 'Limousin' from the St Dizier wing parked at Waddington. French 'tin nose' Jaguars are remarkably austere compared to their RAF counterparts, lacking the laser ranger, navigation and weapons aiming system (NAVWASS), projected map display (PMD), and electronic counter-measures (ECM) installation fitted to the British GR.1 and export versions. The French Jaguar has also missed out on the uprated Adour 804 turbofans retrofitted to RAF aircraft. The nearest Jag, serial A79 '7-NP', is equipped with a practice bomb dispenser on the centreline pylon

Jaguar groundcrew prepare to load chaff cannisters into the *PHIMAT* pod under the outer pylon on the right wing. The crewman in the centre holds the loading rod used to push the chaff tubes into the pod

Afterburners glowing, a Jaguar A accelerates down the runway. French Jaguars have seen action during the civil war in Chad against pro-Libyan rebels and a number have been lost to ground fire. The air force operates 123 of the A (*Appui Tactique*) model and 36 two-seat E (*École de Combat*) trainers

The French Air Force also provided air defence assets at TFM 86 in the form of two Mirage F.1Cs from EC 2/30, the famous 'Normandie-Niemen' squadron based at Istres. This unit, originally formed in Syria in September 1942, achieved legendary success fighting the *Luftwaffe* on the Russian Front in WW2 flying Yakovlev Yak-3s and −9s. The Mirage F.1C is an outstanding interceptor and it has the ability to manoeuvre very well in a low speed fight thanks to combat flaps. In intercept configuration, the F.1C is typically armed with a single radar-guided Matra Super 530 missile on the centreline and two wingtip-mounted Matra 550 Magic infrared homing dogfight missiles; two 30 mm DEFA 5−53 cannon are fixed in the forward fuselage, each with 135 rounds

Like the RAF, the French Air Force use the probe-
and-drogue method for inflight refuelling.
Relatively few missions need an airborne top-up
and many tactical aircraft have detachable probes
to save space and money — the Mirage is no
exception. A fleet of 11 Boeing C-135s provide the
necessary tanker support as required. The
zero-zero ejection seat is a Martin-Baker F.10M

Swept battle formation: Mirage pilots often enter combat with the wingman briefed to keep it tight and stay 'welded wing' on his leader. Unfortunately, if an opposing pilot is switched on he can often get two kills for the price of one

A Hawk's eye view of the NATO Boeing E-3A Sentry which deployed to Waddington from Geilenkirchen in West Germany to provide the TFM with airborne early warning (AEW) cover. Ironically, Waddington was still waiting for the first of its long-promised complement of 11 Nimrod AEW.3s. UK Secretary of State for Defence George Younger subsequently swung the axe on the entire £900 million British project on 18 December 1986. It is clearly beyond the scope of this book to examine the Nimrod AEW fiasco or the relative merits of the two competing systems. Suffice it to say that the RAF has had to make the best of a very bad job and expects to take delivery of its first Boeing AEW.4 in 1990

Overleaf The rare sight of a Sentry cruising at low altitude. On patrol, the aircraft would be flying about 28,000ft (9185 m) higher

Left A perfect plan view of the Sentry, one of 18 operated by NATO. This particular example is registered LX-N90456

Above The business end of an F-15C Eagle, dominated by the radome for its digitized Hughes APG-63 lightweight X-band pulse-Doppler radar.

Right The AIM-9L Sidewinder, recognizable by its 'double delta' control fins, can be launched from virtually any angle with the high probability of a positive kill. In 1982 the 'Nine Lima' established its deadly reputation in the hands of British Sea Harrier pilots in the Falklands conflict, and the 'turkey shoot' of poorly flown Syrian MiGs over the Bekaa Valley in Lebanon by Israeli F-15s and F-16s

Preceding pages Eagles from the 1st TFW based at Langley, Virginnia, rise to command the air on a CAP mission

Left Courtesy of the Optica observation aircraft which attended the concurrent industry exhibition at TFM 86, this aspect of two F-15Cs from the 36th TFW at Bitburg in West Germany is strangely similar to American spy satellite images of the MiG-29 taken at the Ramenskoye test centre near Moscow. The F-15 has a large reflective area and makes a good radar target. Its sheer size can also be a handicap if the combat closes to visual range, but the 'flying tennis court' still seems to cope with all-comers. The industry exhibition was very welcome and gave aircrew the chance to button-

hole manufacturers to obtain technical data and discuss any problems. Industry also contributed generously to the social programme. Mine's a pint!

Above The Canadian Armed Forces sent four CF-188s from No 439 Sqn at Baden-Sollingen in West Germany to TFM 86, but this Hornet was photographed at Binbrook in early 1986

Generation gap: the sleek Hornet tries to put the ageing Lightning in the shade as it taxies out for takeoff. The CF-188 is not referred to as the Hornet (officially anyway) because the name isn't bilingual. Canada is taking delivery of 98 CF-188 strike fighters and 40 CF-188D operational trainers

Right The Hornet's naval pedigree is revealed by its hefty landing gear, designed to absorb the punishment of violent deck landings. Other key features include the huge leading edge extensions (LEX), Hughes APG-65 multi-mode radar, nose-mounted M61A1 Vulcan 20 mm cannon with 540 rounds, and smokeless General Electric F404−400 turbofans of 16,000 lb (7257 kg) thrust each with afterburner

The Canadians visited Binbrook to polish up their air combat manoeuvring (ACM) skills, having already made the grade in the air-to-ground game. The spoof canopy painted on the underside — a Canadian innovation — is designed to confuse opponents and the effect can turn the tables in a split second. Most of us Lightning pilots were pleased to have a crack at the Hornet — it really is an excellent fighting machine. We couldn't resist swopping notes with the Canadians on our encounters with the ultimate dogfighter, the Fighting Falcon. How does the Hornet compare? One of their pilots declared that 'flying combat against the F-16 is like having a knife fight in a telephone box!'

Nearly airborne after a very short takeoff run, a Hornet heads into the void. Nos 409, 421, and 439 Sqns in West Germany have all converted to the Hornet from the CF-104 Starfighter

Gear up, positive climb: the same aircraft departs
Binbrook for an area familiarization (sector recce)
sortie

A German Navy Tornado maritime strike aircraft of *Marinefliegerschwader* 1 being put through its paces by Capt Richie Bensch in May 1986. The *Marineflieger* is taking delivery of 96 Tornados to replace the F-104G Starfighter, a process which should be complete when the second strike wing, MFG 2, is declared operational at the end of 1987. **Left** Richie Bensch exercises the refuelling probe

In operational configuration *Marineflieger* Tornados are armed with Kormoran anti-ship missiles and/or HARMs to neutralize naval radars. The missile mix may also include AIM-9L Sidewinders for self-defence to bolster the aircraft's two internal 27 mm Mauser cannon (125 rounds apiece). A BOZ-101 chaff and flare dispenser would normally be carried on each outboard wing pylon. *Marineflieger* Tornados are also equipped to carry a reconnaissance pod

Left The Vikings, the *Marineflieger's* dynamic Starfighter display team, catch up with Richie Bench's Tornado after one of their final performances at the Mildenhall Open Day in 1986. Sadly, the Vikings disbanded later that year and the airshow circuit will be poorer for their passing. Few people will forget their rip-roaring routines and the howling note of the old '104

Above After that brief interlude with the German Navy Tornado, we are back at TFM 86. The distinctive badge on the intake reveals that this F-4F Phantom is from the *Luftwaffe's* senior fighter wing, JG 71 'Richthofen' at Wittmundhafen. The pilot's ladder is in the extended position

117

Back at Binbrook again, but staying with German Phantoms, a Neuberg-based F-4F interceptor from JG 74 'Mölders' displays mucho macho. The *Luftwaffe* is currently planning its second F-4 upgrade programme and roughly 74 F-4Fs will be retrofitted with Hughes APG-65 radar, new avionics, digital IFF, and AMRAAM capability. All being well, the Eurofighter is expected to replace British, German, and Spanish Phantoms in the air defence role from about 1996

Parked on Binbrook's aircraft servicing pan (ASP), a Sidewinder AIM-9L-armed F-4F of JG 74, coded 37+80, is being readied for a sortie in the winter of 1985. The fairing under the nose houses the 20 mm M61A1 cannon introduced on the air force F-4E and also fitted to the Japanese F-4EJ

Left Afterburner plumes licking the winter air, F-4F Phantoms of JG 74 thrust skywards from Runway 03. The two-tone paint job (top) is now standard on F-4F interceptors

Above Phantom FG.1s of No 43 Sqn ('The Fighting Cocks') based at RAF Leuchars in Scotland formed part of the air defence assets of No 11 Group tasked with engaging the large 'force packages' (up to 70 aircraft) launched from Waddington at TFM 86. Wing folding is a Phantom characteristic, a throwback to the original US Navy requirement to maximize the available parking space on crowded carrier decks

Overleaf A pristine Phantom FG.1 (F-4K) of No 43 Sqn (XV590/X) flown by ex-Lightning pilot Sqn Ldr John Cliffe. All good things come to an end I guess, and *somebody* has to fly it, but the F-4 is a rock of an aeroplane compared to the knife sharp Lightning. Seriously, though, the long-legged F-4 represents an enormous advance over the Lightning, particularly in terms of combat persistence: 4 × Sky Flash and 4 × Sidewinder AIM-9L versus 2 × Firestreak or Red Top = no contest. Due to escalating fatigue damage, RAF F-4K/M Phantoms will be re-winged by British Aerospace to extend the aircraft's service life into the 1990s. Four F-4 squadrons will supplant the Tornado ADV force until the first Eurofighter units become operational

Above Armed with a live Sky Flash missile under the belly, a Tornado F.2 (serial ZD941/AU) from No 229 OCU at RAF Coningsby in Lincolnshire, cruises at medium altitude with its swing-wings swept in the intermediate 45-degree position

Right The same aircraft, crewed by Flt Lt Paul Burnside and navigator Sqn Ldr Andy Lister-Tomlinson, paces a Jindivik drone piloted by operators at RAE Llanbedr in North Wales. Powered by a Viper Mk 201 turbojet, the Jindivik is equipped to tow infrared and radar targets designed to attract both air-to-air and surface-to-air missiles